Schwerpunktthema
Abitur Englisch

Billy Elliot
A Film Study

W0277427

Cornelsen

S. Laing

Billy Elliot A Film Study

von Sabine Struß

Verlagsredaktion
Dr. Marion Kiffe, Christine Finke (Assistenz), Dr. Ilka Soennecken (Bild- und Textrechte)

Layoutkonzept
Annika Preyhs für Buchgestaltung+, Berlin

Technische Umsetzung
Petra Eberhard Grafik Design, Berlin

Umschlaggestaltung
hawemannundmosch, Konzeption und Gestaltung, Berlin

www.cornelsen.de

1. Auflage, 1. Druck 2013

Alle Drucke dieser Auflage sind inhaltlich unverändert und können im Unterricht nebeneinander verwendet werden.

Druck: H. Heenemann, Berlin

ISBN 978-3-06-033438-4

Inhalt gedruckt auf säurefreiem Papier aus nachhaltiger Forstwirtschaft.

POST-VIEWING ACTIVITIES

EXAM TASKS

FILM STUDIES: EXTRAS

ACKNOWLEDGEMENTS

Dear student,

A lot of critics regard *Billy Elliot* as a feel-good-movie. This is definitely true, considering its rousing atmosphere and the energy and the stamina with which eleven-year-old Billy Elliot pursues his dreams and finally succeeds.

Still, the film has its sad and thought-provoking moments – the clash between the police and the rioters, the miners' strike, or Jackie destroying his wife's piano. These moments combined with a wide range of themes in the film offer many topics for discussion in the classroom. Not only can most of its viewers identify with Billy clinging to his dreams against the resistance of his father and brother, some of them may even have experienced gender stereotypes or class differences; they may have struggled with the generation gap or been able to overcome ideas and values they were once convinced of.

In addition to this, the film offers a lot more: it is set in a mining village against the background of the 1984 Miners' Strike. Understanding the historical and cultural background on the one hand helps to understand the clash of values in the film and, on the other hand, gives us insight into a political era in the UK that continues to shape the country's development to this very day.

Last but not least, there is a large variety of filmic devices to be observed that skilfully underline the action in several scenes. The impressive and powerful images might also help you to cope with the Northern English dialect. If you still have problems understanding much of what is said, try watching the film with the English subtitles turned on.

This booklet contains information on the film, including a list of questions for different stages of your work. The pre-viewing activities help you to get an idea of what to expect from the movie. The while-viewing tasks begin with a list of quotations that give you an overview of the storyline. You will then find tasks that concentrate on various aspects of the content, as well as on the way certain ideas are presented in terms of filmmaking. The post-viewing tasks provide additional background information and suggest topics for more general discussions. The FILM STUDIES: EXTRAS at the end might be useful in many ways when working with this booklet.

Moreover, the booklet also contains a variety of different assignments, i.e. comprehension, analysis, and comment, as well as listening and reading tasks, creative tasks and tasks that involve a lot of speaking or interaction so that you can improve different skills throughout your study of the film.

The critic Steve Warren once wrote, "*Billy Elliot* has an obvious appeal to anyone who felt different growing up, but its spirit should reach even the small minority who don't fit the latter category." I hope you enjoy the movie (as well as the various assignments in this booklet)!

Sabine Struß

BILLY ELLIOT

Directed by	Stephen Daldry	**Starring**	Jamie Bell
Written by	Lee Hall		Julie Walters
Produced by	Charles Brand		Jean Heywood

THE PLOT

Eleven-year-old Billy Elliot lives with his father, Jackie, his older brother, Tony, and his senile grandmother in a mining village in the north east of England. Billy's mother died some time ago. The story is set in the 1980s and Jackie and Tony, both miners, are on strike, which makes it hard for the family to make ends meet.

Jackie pays Billy 50p every week to go to boxing lessons, but Billy soon finds out that boxing does not suit him and attends a ballet class instead. When Jackie finds out, the whole family is put to the test. Despite Billy's obvious talent and the offer of his ballet teacher, Mrs Wilkinson, to give him private training, Billy's father and brother are strictly opposed to Billy doing ballet because they consider it inappropriate for boys. Only his friend Michael, Mrs Wilkinson's daughter Debbie and Billy's grandmother seem to understand him. The conflict comes to a head when Billy misses an audition for the Royal Ballet School because of Tony being in trouble with the police.

When Jackie accidentally walks in on Billy dancing for his friend Michael in the gym at night he is overwhelmed and realizes Billy's potential. The prospect of a better future for Billy finally makes him come to terms with his stereotypes. Jackie leaves no stone unturned to give Billy a chance. He even pawns his wife's jewellery, becomes a strike-breaker and convinces Tony of Billy's talent. With support from the family and the other miners the Elliots manage to raise enough money to travel to London for an audition at the Royal Ballet School.

While there, Billy nearly wants to back out when he becomes aware of class distinctions and cultural differences, but in the end he succeeds and becomes a professional ballet dancer.

SCENE INDEX

Chapter (Time)	Characters/Action
1 0:00 – 6:04	**Main Titles**
	At home in the morning, Billy puts on a record and starts jumping to the song "I was dancing when I was twelve". He prepares breakfast for his demented grandmother and is apparently in a good mood, even though he has to run out of the house to search for his grandmother. She seems disorientated and wanders around on a field in the neighbourhood. In the background police can be seen. At night, Billy's brother Tony, who shares a room with Billy, finds out that Billy has been playing his records. The next morning, Billy practises playing the piano, which annoys his father; Tony wants his father to hurry up to join the strikers; their grandmother is still in bed.
2 6:04 – 8:00	**A Disgrace to the Gloves**
	A confrontation between police and strikers can be seen. Billy goes to his boxing lesson in a gym in which ballet classes are held as well. Billy's father has come to watch Billy box, but Billy performs a kind of dance in the ring instead of boxing properly and is knocked down. Consequently, Billy has to practise with the punch bag.
3 8:00 – 13:55	**The Ballet Class**
	After the boxing lesson, Billy is alone in the gym with the ballet class. He feels attracted by the music and the dancing and watches the ballet class. After a while he joins in. While he is walking home, Mrs Wilkinson, the ballet teacher, drives by and asks Billy to pay 50p for the lesson. Having arrived at home, Billy and his grandmother go to his mother's grave and talk about dancing. At night, Billy wants to talk about death with his brother Tony, but Tony refuses to talk.
4 13:55 – 22:02	**To Be a Dancer**
	Billy and Debbie, Mrs Wilkinson's daughter, pass by a police cordon on their way to school, which does not impress them at all. At home in the afternoon, Billy plays the piano again. Later he joins the ballet class instead of attending the boxing lesson. After the lesson, Mrs Wilkinson has a word with Billy about the importance of regular attendance. Coming home, Billy sneaks in and tries to hide the ballet shoes. He is interrupted by his father, who wants Billy to take good care of his grandfather's boxing gloves. The next day at school, Billy is constantly thinking of dancing and is daydreaming in the lesson. A little later, the class is running outside and Billy and his friend Michael skip parts of the cross-country run and talk about ballet. In the afternoon, Billy wants to borrow a ballet book from the library bus. When he is not allowed to take it on his junior ticket, he steals it. Home again, he locks himself in his bedroom and practises moves from the book. Finally he succeeds in the ballet lesson and is shown running and dancing joyfully on his way home.

Chapter (Time)	Characters/Action
5 22:02 – 32:08	**Dad Finds Out**
	During the protest against strike-breakers outside the mine, the boxing coach, George, tells Billy's father, Jackie, that Billy does not show up at boxing any more. In the supermarket Tony and Jackie confront Tony's best mate, who has joined the strike-breakers. At home again, Jackie wants to find out what Billy does during the boxing lessons but Billy hurries out carrying his gloves and hiding his ballet shoes in his trousers. Jackie goes to the gym to check whether Billy still attends the boxing lessons and finds him dancing in the midst of the girls. He forces Billy to come home with him. They discuss whether ballet is appropriate for boys and in the end, Jackie forbids Billy to go to either class. Billy calls his father a bastard and runs out angrily.
6 32:08-36:42	**Mrs Wilkinson's Offer**
	Billy walks through a middle-class neighbourhood in search of the Wilkinsons' house. Once inside, Mrs Wilkinson encourages Billy to stand up to his father. They have dinner together. Billy and Debbie go upstairs and talk openly about their parents, which leads to a certain degree of intimacy between them. Mrs Wilkinson finally gives Billy a lift home and offers to give him private lessons for free in order to prepare him for the Royal Ballet School audition. The next day Billy visits Michael, who is wearing a dress when he opens the door. Inside both talk about the things they like and their plans for the future (e.g. being a ballet dancer).
7 36:42-46:09	**Private Lessons**
	For the next dancing lesson, Billy brings along objects that are important to him. They are to serve as inspiration for a dance. Among them is a letter from his mother, which Billy knows by heart. Based on his experiences and emotions, Billy and Mrs Wilkinson create a dance. After the lesson, Billy walks home. At 4:00 a.m. the next morning, Tony intends to leave the house to take illegal measures to enforce the strike. Jackie disapproves of Tony's ideas. They argue and when Tony accuses his dad of having been useless since his wife died, Jackie knocks him down. Billy eavesdrops and is sad about the whole situation. At the next dancing lesson Mrs Wilkinson tells Billy off because he hasn't practised. They argue and in the end, she slaps him. Soon they both regret what they have said and done and find comfort in each other. Afterwards they continue practising.
8 46:09-52:04	**A Ghost Story**
	Billy and Mrs Wilkinson are on their way to a performance of *Swan Lake* when Billy finds a classical music tape in Mrs Wilkinson's car. The tune seems familiar to him and Mrs Wilkinson tells him the story of Swan Lake. Back at home Billy peeps into his grandmother's bedroom to see if she is all right and has a vision of his mother in the kitchen. This vision makes him realize that his mum would have supported him. On the next day in the gym, Billy and Mrs Wilkinson concentrate on the improvement of his performance. In the changing room after the class, Debbie and Billy talk about dancing and Debbie says she will miss him if he is accepted at the audition.

Chapter (Time)	Characters/Action
9 52:04 – 55:50	**Tony's Arrest**
	There is a clash between the police and rioters: Tony is chased through the neighbourhood and finally beaten up and arrested by the police. Billy observes the whole scene. The next morning, Billy phones Mrs Wilkinson to tell her that he can't come to the audition, but Debbie puts down the receiver. Later, Billy and Jackie arrive at the court to take Tony home. At the same time Mrs Wilkinson is waiting for Billy in the gym and finally decides to go to Billy's house.
10 55:50 – 1:01:22	**The Chance to Dance**
	When the Elliots arrive back at their house, Billy tries to ignore his ballet teacher. Tony is quite aggressive towards her, but Jackie invites her to come in. When Tony hears of the missed audition, he accuses Mrs Wilkinson of making a twat of Billy, of being snobbish, unqualified and only interested in her own gratification. Billy can't stand the argument, runs out into the backyard and feels trapped. Jackie looks angry, but behaves passively. Billy dances through the streets, watched by different people.
11 1:01:22 – 1:04:44	**Christmas**
	In the miners' social club, the striking workers and their families celebrate Christmas (funded by charity money). At home, Jackie destroys his wife's piano because he needs the wood to heat their house. While the family is celebrating Christmas, Jackie becomes emotional. A little later Billy and Michael build a snowman in the street. Billy finds out that Michael is homosexual.
12 1:04:44 – 1:08:37	**Dance of Defiance**
	Billy takes Michael to the gym, gives him a tutu to wear and shows him some steps. Some drunken miners, among them Jackie, come home from the pub, pass the gym, hear the music and go inside. Jackie sees Billy (and Michael in his tutu), but before Jackie can explode with anger, Billy starts dancing. Finally, Jackie leaves without a word, Michael applauds and Billy follows his father, who tells him to go home.
13 1:08:37 – 1:17:14	**Dad's Decision**
	On the next day Jackie is on his way to the Wilkinsons. He wants to see Mrs Wilkinson to ask her about the fees for the Royal Ballet School and they talk about an audition in London. Jackie feels offended by Mrs Wilkinson's offer to pay the fare to London. At home, Billy is still awake. When Jackie comes home, he sits down on Billy's bed, pondering his son's future. Jackie finally decides to join the strike-breakers because he needs the money to support Billy. The next morning, Tony sees him on the bus that takes the miners to the mine. Tony climbs over the fence and runs after his father, who explains his decision. Both start crying because they don't know how to support Billy. At night in the boys' bedroom, Tony tells Billy that he agrees with his father about Billy's future. George offers to give back all the 50p coins he got for the boxing lessons in order to support Billy's trip to the audition. Jackie decides to pawn his wife's jewellery. Eventually, Billy and Jackie are on their way to the bus. Billy wants to know about London and learns that Jackie has never made it past Durham.

Chapter (Time)	Characters/Action
14 1:17:14 – 1:23:00	**The Audition**
	At the Royal Ballet School, Billy is listed as William Elliot at the reception desk, which confuses him. When he is examined, the doctor calls him William again. The whole situation makes him want to leave, but Jackie does not accept withdrawal. Billy is very nervous, performs his dance and is sent out by the board without any comments. He is frustrated and smacks a boy who wants to comfort him in the changing room.
15 1:23:00 – 1:27:00	**The Interview**
	Jackie and Billy are called in and admonished for the incident in the changing room. In the interview, Billy does not know any answers to the board's questions. When he is just about to leave the room, he is asked a final question about his feelings while dancing. After initial difficulties to express himself, he comes up with some emotional descriptions.
16 1:27:00 – 1:37:42	**The Letter**
	Home again, Billy and Jackie wait for the letter. Billy can't concentrate at school and on his way home from school, George wishes him good luck. At the same time, the letter is being delivered. Tony, Billy's grandmother and Jackie are sitting around the table, having placed the letter in the middle. Billy enters the kitchen, but prefers to read the letter privately. In his room Billy opens the letter and seems quite moved. His family can't wait to hear about the content of the letter. When they enter the room, they find Billy crying about his acceptance to the Royal Ballet School. Jackie runs out on the street, storms into the miners' social club shouting out the good news, but some of his friends hardly react and let him know that the union caved in and that the strike is over. Later, Billy and Jackie sit on a fence at the cemetery talking about Billy's future and laugh together. Billy goes to the gym once again to say thank you and goodbye to Mrs Wilkinson; at home he says goodbye to his grandmother. Tony and his father accompany Billy to the bus. On the way to the bus station, Michael shouts after them. Billy runs back and kisses him goodbye. At the bus station, Jackie heartily embraces Billy before he enters the bus. From outside Tony says that he'll miss him, but Billy can only see him gesturing. While Billy is on his way, life goes on in Everington. The miners are back to work.
17 1:37:42 – 1:40:27	**Billy's Big Night**
	Several years later, Jackie and Tony are on their way to a performance of *Swan Lake* in London. In the theatre they meet Michael, who says he wouldn't have missed this performance for anything in the world. Jackie and Tony let Billy know that his family have come to watch him. When the performance starts, Jackie is close to tears.
18 1:40:27 – 1:45:50	**End Titles**

QUESTIONS ON THE FILM

Before watching the film, you might wish to consider these questions:

1 What is your opinion about films that include a lot of music and dancing?

2 Which aspects of the film seem most interesting to you?

3 In what way do you think the setting of the film will be related to its storyline?

4 Do you think striking is an effective way of influencing politics? Say why (not).

5 In what ways might children's plans for the future be different from what parents hope or expect?

The following questions might be interesting while viewing the film:

6 How does Billy express emotion in the film? How does his family express emotion?

7 Which scenes in the film are particularly humorous or ironic?

8 How is music included in the film? In which scenes does music play an essential role?

9 What is your impression of everyday life in Everington, County Durham?

10 Several scenes were filmed in the same street: it is lined by rows of houses and it leads to the sea and a blue sky. In what way does this setting underline the action?

After watching the film, you can possibly deal with these questions:

11 What is your impression of the filming technique in general? Are there any predominant techniques or images that stuck in your mind?

12 Which people influence Billy most?

13 How are class distinctions presented in the film?

14 What is the message of the film?

15 Most major characters in the film are male. In what way do they influence Billy or function as role models?

16 What role do the female characters play for Billy? In what way does his mother still influence him and his family?

17 Would you recommend the film to a friend? Why or why not?

PRE-VIEWING ACTIVITIES

What to Expect? – A Think-Pair-Share Activity

Think: Ballet and mining play an important role in the movie. What do you associate with these two words? Write down as many ideas as possible for each cluster.

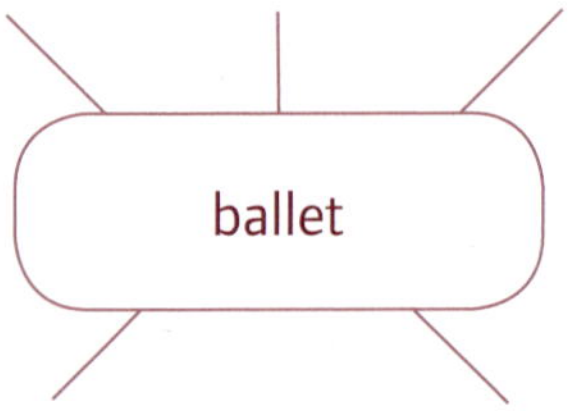

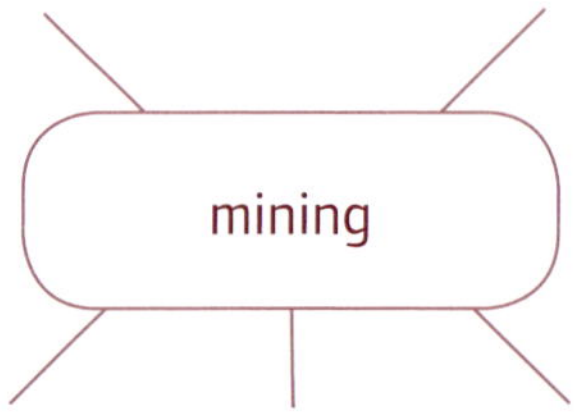

Pair: Present your ideas to a partner. Then try to describe the contrast between the two words in no more than three sentences.

Share: Now share the results from your pair work in class.

Useful vocabulary:

... can be related to ...
I associate ... with ...
... is (closely) connected with...
... makes me think of ...
... reminds me of ...
in contrast to ...
while/whereas...
on the one hand ... on the other hand ...

A Film Poster

1 Describe the poster in detail. What could the film be about?

2 What might the boy and the girls be thinking in that particular situation? Write a speech bubble for the boy and one girl expressing their thoughts.

3 Would you like to watch the film?
Why or why not?

Useful vocabulary:

The film might/could be about ...
There might/could be ...
... possibly ...
It is likely that ...
I guess ...
It seems as if ...

The Correct Order

1 While watching the film, put the chapter headings from the DVD in the correct order. Fill in the table and explain each title in one sentence.

a The Chance to Dance
b The Audition
c Dad's Decision
d The Ballet Class
e Mrs Wilkinson's Offer
f Christmas
g Dad Finds Out
h To Be a Dancer
i A Disgrace to the Gloves
j Tony's Arrest
k Private Lessons
l The Interview
m A Dance of Defiance
n The Letter
o A Ghost Story
p Billy's Big Night

Position	Chapter	Explanation
1		
2		
3		
4		
5		
6		
7		
8		
9		
10		
11		
12		
13		
14		
15		
16		

WHILE-VIEWING ACTIVITIES

Who Said What to Whom?

When watching the movie for the first time, try and explain the meaning of the following quotes from the movie: who said what to whom and in what situation?

1 Walk normal, will you?

2 Don't pick on me because you fucked up your own life.

3 Glad to see you've come to your senses.

4 I feel like a right sissy.

5 He's been made redundant.

6 I never made it past Durham.

7 First rule of the union, Gary: you never cross a picket line.

8 But once I get going I forget everything. I sort of disappear.

9 This is man-to-man combat, not a bloody tea dance.

10 Do you think being a ballet dancer would be better than being a miner?

11 You know exactly what's wrong with it.

12 It's just a few commies, stirring things up.

13 Aren't you a bit old?

14 You should stand up to him.

15 Since Mom died you are nothing but a useless twat.

16 This is when you go out and find life.

17 I wouldn't have missed it for the world.

Music Makes the World Go Round

Discuss with a partner:

1 Which role do music and dancing play for you personally?

2 Which dancing scenes from the movie did you like best or remember best? Explain why.

Watch the beginning of the movie [00:00:38 – 00:02:30].

3 Describe the atmosphere created in this sequence.

Useful vocabulary:

The music contributes to / creates a ... atmosphere.
The atmosphere can be described as...
a joyous/warm/cold/cheerful/peaceful/tender/tense/happy/angry/hopeful/energetic/light-hearted/gloomy/idyllic/nostalgic/playful/romantic/fanciful/mysterious/suspenseful/sorrowful/melancholy/sentimental/frightening/ ... atmosphere

4 Explain how Billy responds to the music. In what way does this hint at the relevance that music and dancing have in the film?

5 Read the infobox below, then analyse the use of music in this sequence.

INFOBOX | **Music**

In films, the source of music (or sounds in general) may be part of the story (= diegetic) or added on (= non-diegetic). With diegetic sound, its source can be visible (= on-screen) or unseen (= off-screen).

Of course, any kind of music can be used in films – from classical or traditional music to rock, punk or disco music. It may come across as exotic or familiar.

Music is normally not used in films simply as adornment. Rather, it is used as an extra channel of information alongside the images: it may e.g. intensify or support the action shown. It may comment on it by foreshadowing things that will happen later or by contradicting the images shown. Music can direct the viewer's attention within the image or it can shape our interpretation of the image.

When analysing the use of music in a film, it is important to examine its relationship to the images and to define its purpose.

6 Read the lyrics of the song that accompanies the sequence. In what way could they be related to the sequence?

T-Rex: Cosmic Dancer

I was dancing when I was twelve
I was dancing when I was aaah
I danced myself right out the womb
Is it strange to dance so soon
I danced myself right out the womb

I was dancing when I was eight
Is it strange to dance so late?
I danced myself into the tomb
Is it strange to dance so soon?
I danced myself into the tomb

Is it wrong to understand
The fear that dwells inside a man?
What's it like to be a loon
I liken it to a balloon

I danced myself out of the womb
Is it strange to dance so soon
I danced myself into the tomb
But when again once more

I danced myself out of the womb
Is it strange to dance so soon
I danced myself out of the womb.

[00:02:24]

7 Identify other filmic devices used in the sequence and describe their function.

8 **Mediation:** A friend of yours is not very good at English. He has seen Billy Elliot in German, but still doesn't understand the lyrics of the songs in the film. Briefly summarize the lyrics of "Cosmic Dancer" for him in German and explain the relationship between the lyrics and the first scenes of the film.

The Main Characters: a Group Puzzle

[00:38:44]

[00:32:52]

[00:23:37]

[00:26:25]

Billy, Mrs Wilkinson, Tony and Jackie Elliot can be regarded as the major characters in the film. While watching the film, collect information about them so that you can describe each character in detail.

Expert Groups: Read the infobox below. Divide the class into four groups. Each group describes the character of one person from the film. Everybody must make notes!

Be careful to consider the following aspects in your characterization:

- facts, family background and outward appearance
- the character's behaviour and interactions
- their attitudes, beliefs, values and feelings.

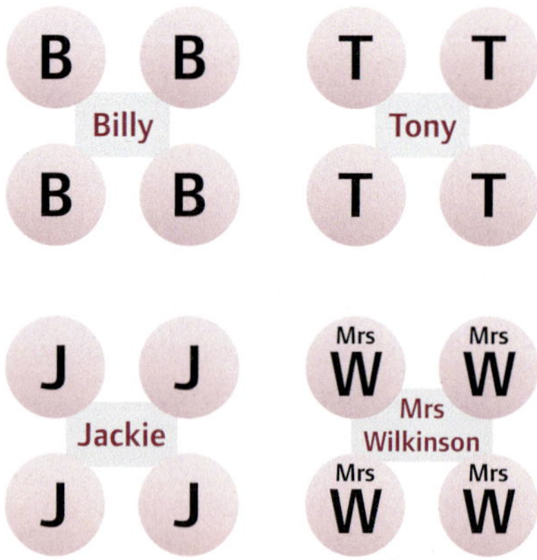

INFOBOX	Characterization in Films

Characters can be presented in various ways. In films, viewers can gain an understanding of a character by observing the character's behaviour, interactions, language, body language, facial expression, taste, clothing, etc.

Secondly, they are characterized by other characters; one character might think or talk about another character.

Thirdly, cinematic devices often contribute to the way the character is seen by the audience. Field size, shot and point of view, music, sound or light effects often influence a viewer's perception.

Mixed Groups: Form mixed groups, so that your new groups have an "expert" for each character. Present your findings to each other.

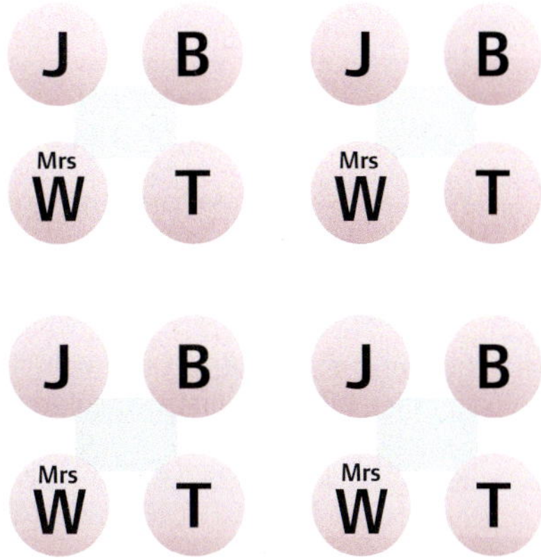

Additional task: After having learned about each character, use the information to visualize the character constellation of the film on a poster, i.e. draw a diagram in which you arrange the characters according to their relationships to others (cf. the infobox below). Use labeled arrows to indicate their relationship. Include Billy, Billy's family, and Mrs Wilkinson and perhaps even Michael and Debbie in your chart.

Useful vocabulary:

rather negative	⟷	**rather positive**
look down on sb.	tolerate sb.	have (great) respect for sb.
regard sb. with contempt	be indifferent to sb./sth.	have a lot in common with sb.
be afraid of sb.	feel uneasy about sb.	admire sb.
show disrespect for sb.	feel sympathy for sb.	be fascinated by sb.
disagree with sb.	protect sb.	be in love with sb.
despise sb. for sth.	be strict with sb.	be fond of sb.
criticize sb. for sth.	accept sb.	get on well with sb.
		look up to sb.
		care for sb.
		support/defend sb.

Presentation: Present your posters to the class. You may put up the posters in your classroom and organize a gallery walk: get together in your expert groups again and stroll from poster to poster. Each poster must be presented by a student who helped to make it.

INFOBOX | Character Constellation

The constellation of characters shows the relationships between the characters of a story. It can remain relatively stable or may change in the course of a film (or book). Often the character constellation can best be displayed graphically.

You can use different types of lines to demonstrate the system of relationships or you can label lines and arrows. Use a dictionary to find appropriate vocabulary.

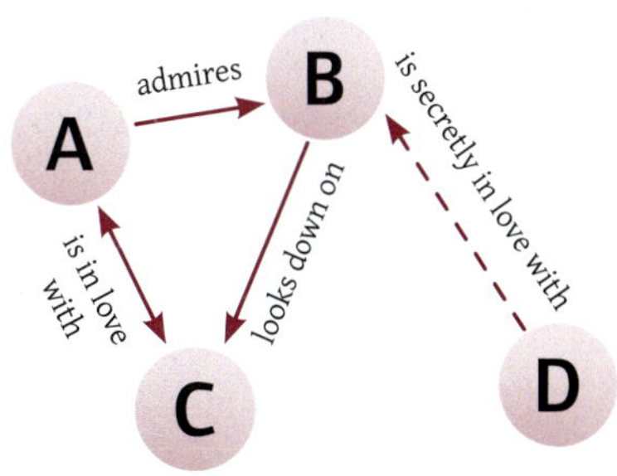

⚠ Streit w. teacher & family in KLA

Mixed Images

Starke Fixierung auf cinematic devices

Watch [00:19:16 – 00:21:08], [00:22:04 – 00:23:13] and [00:40:13 – 00:41:21].

In these sequences, music and dancing play an important role. Additionally, the shots in these sequences are put together in a particular way to achieve a certain effect.

1 Watch the sequences closely. Describe the setting and the plot, and identify elements that help link the shots in the sequences (activities, words, symbols, etc.). If necessary, copy the table, then fill in the first two columns.

2 Watch the sequence again. Identify cinematic devices used (used to link the shots) and analyse their effect. You may consult FILM STUDIES: EXTRAS (see p. 47). Fill in the last column.
↳ nur editing terms (wenn überhaupt) relevant

Setting and Plot	Linking Elements =Montage/ Editing	~~Cinematic Devices~~ and Their Effects
Scene 1 [00:19:16 – 00:21:08]		
Billy practicing the pirouette at different places		
Scene 2 [00:22:04 – 00:23:13]		
Mrs Wilkinson giving dancing instructions that match Billy's movements & the strikers' movements		

Es: Im Englischen werden Analysis & Interpretation nicht so scharf getrennt.

Setting and Plot	Linking Elements	~~Cinematic Devices and~~ Their Effects
Scene 3 [00:40:13 – 00:41:21]		
Mrs Wilkinson & Billy creating a boogie dance that (subconsciously) seems to be contaging his (innocent) family members		

3 Read the Infobox below. Examine in what way the montage of the three scenes helps to create a certain atmosphere. Write a text of about 250 words. = "linking atmosphere

INFOBOX	Montage and Editing

Montage is the technique of arranging shots in a film sequence. Montage creates a sensible and meaningful relationship between the individual shots and is one of the most important tools to tell a story and create particular effects.

eher hinterher

Useful vocabulary:

the sequence	consists of	alternating medium shots of... a rapid succession of shots showing ... a juxtaposition of ...
the scene presents	a close-up of ... a medium/long shot of ...	
the camera	cuts from ... to ...	to emphasize that their actions are simultaneous to illustrate the similarities to contrast ... with ...
the music the sound the words	underline(s) ... create(s) an atmosphere of ... support(s) ...	

A Clash of Values

Watch [00:24:50 – 00:27:38].

1 Compare Jackie's and Billy's attitudes towards ballet.

2 Comment on Jackie's reservations.

3 After the quarrel, Billy runs out on the street. In the background, the song "The Children of the Revolution" is playing. What might Billy be thinking? Write his interior monologue (cf. the infobox below).

00:28:06

INFOBOX	Interior Monologue
An interior monologue is a passage of writing that presents a character's thoughts, impressions and feelings as if directly overheard by the audience.	

4 Have you ever experienced situations in which your parents disliked your hobbies or disagreed with you about your plans for the future? Say how you solved your problem.

5 Describe the film still above (cf. FILM STUDIES: EXTRAS, p. 56) and examine in what way the combination of different filmic devices underlines the message of this particular sequence. Consider the camera angle, the camera range, Billy's surroundings, and the use of colour and music.

6 Have a look at the table below. Outline the differences in participation in the various sports between men and women in the UK.

Participation in sport by sex

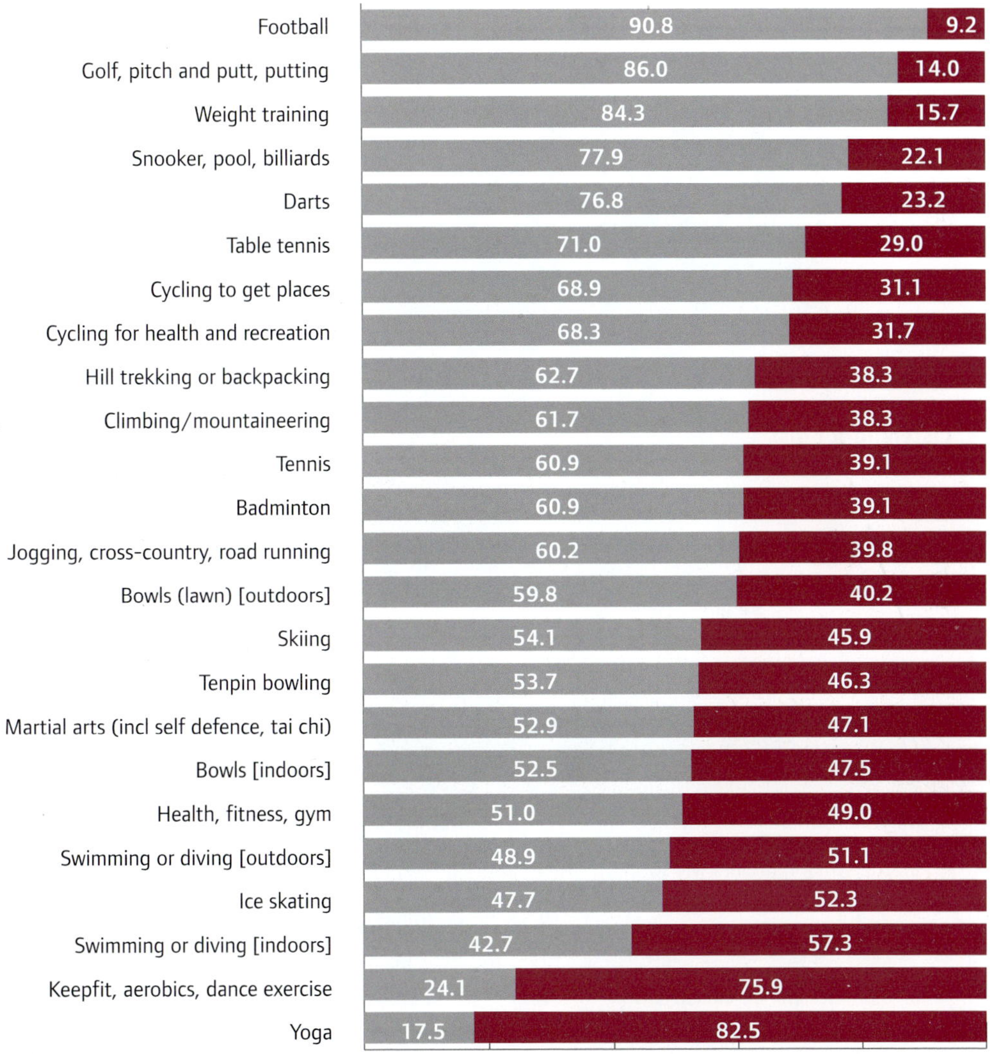

From: Department for culture, media and sport: Adult Participation in Sport *(2011)*

7 Comment on the results: which results do you find striking or surprising? Which numbers might be similar to the levels of participation in sport in Germany?

Different Lives? – Close Viewing/Listening

Watch sequence [00:28:40 – 00:32:00].

00:29:44

Listening for gist

1 Which sentence summarizes the sequence best?

a Mrs Wilkinson has invited Billy over for dinner and Billy makes friends with Debbie.

b Billy visits the Wilkinsons in order to talk about ballet and the miners' strike.

c Billy visits the Wilkinsons and learns that they have also got problems in their family.

Listening for detail: multiple choice

Find the correct ending for each sentence. For one sentence there are two correct endings.

2 Mr Wilkinson believes that …

a the striking miners will soon be back to work.

b all miners are communists.

c all mines will be closed soon.

3 Mr Wilkinson …

a is unemployed.

b has retired.

c is unsatisfied with his job.

4 Debbie says that her father …

a was unfaithful to her mom.

b drinks too much alcohol.

c is incapable of having sex.

5 Billy …

a misses his mother very much.

b cannot remember his mother well.

c sometimes feels sad about having lost his mother.

6 Billy says that Debbie's family …

a is tough.

b is crazy.

c is ridiculous.

A Question of Class

1 Find examples from the scene "Different lives" (cf. p. 24) and the film in general that display the class differences between the Elliots and the Wilkinsons.

2 The following dictionary entry from 1992 describes the relevance of class in Britain at the time when *Billy Elliot* is set. Scan the text for features that can be related to the Elliots and the Wilkinsons.

Social Class in Britain

British society is considered to be divided into three main groups of classes – the UPPER CLASS, the MIDDLE CLASS, and the LOWER or WORKING CLASS. This is known as the class system and it is important to know something about it if you want to understand British people and society. Most British people grow up with a deep knowledge and understanding of the class system even if they are not very conscious of it. Most people know which class they belong to and are able to tell which class another person comes from by the way they speak, their clothes, their interests or even the type of food they eat.

Social class is not only about behaviour and attitudes. For example, although many upper class people are rich and may own a lot of land, having a lot of money does not make a person upper class. It is also important to come from a particular kind of family, have friends who are considered suitable, have been to a certain type of PRIVATE SCHOOL and speak with the right kind of ACCENT. There are people who are poor but who do not think of themselves as working class because their family background, education, political opinions, etc. are different to those of most working-class people. Many people do not like the class system but it is impossible to pretend that these differences do not exist or that British people do not sometimes form opinions in this way.

The following tables show some of the typical ways in which differences between the classes can be seen. They may help you understand any jokes or stories which depend on understanding class which you find on television, in newspapers, etc. The information is intended as a general guide and does not represent the opinion of all British people, nor is it intended to encourage you to share the prejudices of British people. Some of the words in the tables below will have more information at their own place in the dictionary.

FOOD

upper class	middle class	working class
Cordon Bleu		bangers & mash
champagne →	→	fish & chips
caviar		pie & chips
smoked salmon		sugar
		salt & vinegar
	health foods	tomato ketchup
	e.g. wholemeal bread	junk food
	foreign food	
	e.g. avocado, pasta →	→
	restaurants	meat & veg
		Chinese & Indian food, especially takeways

EDUCATION

upper class	middle class	working class
Eton, Harrow	grammar school	comprehensive
public school ←	← state school →	→
prep school		
finishing school		
	Oxford	technical college
	Cambridge	
	university	
←	← polytechnic →	→

WORK/JOBS

upper class	middle class	working class
← professional &	white-collar jobs →	blue-collar & manual jobs
judge		
stockbroker	teacher →	→
company director	accountant	miner
	bank manager	mechanic
	doctor	factory worker
MP →		shop assistant
a job in the City →	→	lorry driver
no job because the person is very rich, 'the idle rich'		

HOUSING

upper class	middle class	working class
own several homes	own their own home	council house or council flat (owned or rented) inner city areas
own a stately home	have a second home	
large landowner	semi-detached or detached house in suburbs	
live in Mayfair and Knightsbridge (rich areas of central London)		

LEISURE		
upper class	**middle class**	**working class**
ballet	theatre →	→
opera	cinema →	→
	television	→
	radio →	→
	← art galleries	
	museums	
	radio 4	ITV soap operas,
	BBC 2	e.g. Coronation St
	Channel 4	
		← pubs
	wine bars →	working men's clubs

SPORTS AND GAMES		
upper class	**middle class**	**working class**
polo		football
any sport involving		darts
horses		horse racing
horse racing		bingo
	← skiing	snooker
	← sailing	
	← tennis →	racing pigeons (in the north)
	← cricket →	
	← golf →	
fox hunting		
hunting, shooting and		
fishing		

POLITICS		
upper class	**middle class**	**working class**
Conservative	Conservative	Conservative
	← Labour →	→
	SDP	
	Liberals	
	Green Party	

HOLIDAYS		
upper class	**middle class**	**working class**
	walking holidays	package tours
	Lake District	Benidorm
Mustique	Devon	Costa del Sol
Gstaad	Cornwall	Ibiza
The Caribbean	France	Blackpool
	Tuscany	British seaside
cruises →	camping	caravans
	villas	holiday camps
Orient Express	gites	
	holiday collages	
	← B & B →	→

From: Dictionary of the English Language and Culture. *Longman 1992, p. 1258*

"Fuckin' Ballet" – Listening Comprehension

Watch sequence [00:55:50 – 00:58:19].

1 Listen carefully and fill the gaps.

Mrs W.: Billy?

Billy: Please, Miss. Don't.

Mrs W.: ……………………………………, Billy?

Tony: Who the fuck are you?

Jackie: I think we better go …………………………… .

Mrs W.: I know this might be difficult for you, but today, Billy missed a very important audition.

Tony: Audition?

Mrs W.: For the Royal Ballet School.

Tony: The Royal Ballet?

Mrs W.: School. It's where they teach the ballet.

Tony: You've got to be jokin', love.

Mrs W.: No, I'm …………………………………… .

Tony: Have you any idea ……………………………………? I've been in a fuckin' cell all night … and you come 'round here, talkin' shite. And you … fuckin' ballet! What are you tryin' to do, make him a fuckin' scab for the rest of his life? Look at him. He's ……………………………………, for fuck's sake.

Billy: You've got to start …………………………………… from when you're young.

Tony: Shut it. I'm not havin' any brother of mine …………………… …………………………… like a right twat for your gratification.

Mrs W.: Excuse me. This is not for my gratification.

Tony: How much good's it gonna do him? You're not takin' him away. He's only a bairn. What about givin' him a childhood?

Billy: I don't wanna childhood. I wanna be a ballet dancer.

Tony: And anyway, what do you know about it? What .... have you got?

Mrs W.: Look, I haven't come here to defend meself.

Tony: Well, for all we know, you could be some fuckin' nutter. I'll get the fuckin' social on to you.

Mrs W.: I think you should .... , son.

Tony: Well, you shake and dance? Well, go on, then. Let's see this fuckin' dancin'.

Mrs W.: No, this is .... !

Tony: If you're a fuckin' ballet dancer, then let's be havin' you.

Mrs W.: Don't you dare!

Tony: What sort of a teacher are you, heh? He's got .... Now, you're fuckin' tellin' him not to. Dance you little twat! ... No ... so, piss off. He's not doin' any more fuckin' ballet! And if you go near him again, I'll smack you one, you .... cow.

Mrs W.: You know nothing about me, you sanctimonious little shit! He won't grow up to race whippets, grow leeks or piss his wages up the wall. Listen! He's been with me ...

They continue arguing and Billy runs out.

16 *scab (infml)* worker who refuses to join a strike

23 *bairn (dial)* child

28 *nutter (infml)* mad or eccentric person

40 *sanctimonious* hypocrite, feeling morally superior

41 *whippet* dog breed that is bred for racing

41 *leek* Porree, Lauch

2 Compare Jackie's behaviour in this scene to how he acted when he first found out about Billy's dancing (chapter 5). What might the reasons for his behaviour be?

Continue watching [00:58:19 – 01:01:00].

3 Describe Billy's reaction to the quarrel. How does he feel about the argument?

4 Describe the still below (cf. FILM STUDIES: EXTRAS, p. 56) and analyse the filmic devices that emphasize Billy's emotions.

00:58:52

5 **Mediation:** The pupils' magazine at your school wants to publish an article about conflicts between teenagers and their parents that may result from having different ideas and expectations about life. Outline how the scene above is an example of this kind of conflict within the family.

The Way They Talk

1 Read the excerpt on p. 28 again and analyse the differences in language used by Tony and Mrs Wilkinson. Concentrate on the categories given in the table. Copy it and fill it accordingly.

	Tony	Mrs Wilkinson
Choice of words		
Sentence structure		
Pronunciation		
...		

Making Sacrifices

Watch sequence [01:10:16 – 01:12:00].

1 Describe what is happening.

01:11:38

2 Examine how Jackie's feelings are underlined by filmic devices. You might wish to watch the sequence twice and/or fill in a reading log for this sequence.

Continue watching the sequence [01:12:00 – 01:16:04].

01:14:19

3 Summarize what Jackie says to Tony.

4 Analyse the filmic devices that help to create the emotional atmosphere.

5 How do the other characters in the film try to support Billy?

The Audition

1 Describe the film still. In what way does it foreshadow Billy's feelings at the audition?

01:17:32

Watch sequence [01:17:20 – 01:26:59].

2 Describe how Billy behaves at the audition.

3 Explain his behaviour.

4 Imagine you are Billy. Explain to your father how you felt at the audition, why you slapped the other boy, and how you feel now.

Father and Son

01:32:07

1 Describe the picture and its atmosphere.

Watch sequence [01:28:14 – 01:32:25].

2 Analyse how suspense is created in the first part of the sequence (at the Elliots' house).

3 Explain how the father-son-relationship has changed.

4 Imagine that at the end of this sequence Jackie wants to give Billy advice for the future. What could he say? Write down a piece of advice. All pieces of advice can be presented in a thought tunnel (see the infobox below).

INFOBOX | **Thought Tunnel or Decision Alley**

Whenever a protagonist is caught in a dilemma, there is an opportunity to analyse the situation and give advice or make suggestions. For this purpose the class forms two lines facing each other through which the protagonist walks slowly from one end to the other. He listens to all pieces of advice and at the end states his feelings or makes a decision.

The Ending – Creative Writing

01:28:42

Watch sequence [01:37:45 – 01:40:22].

1 Describe your reaction to the ending of the film.

2 Watch the scene again and analyse the filmic devices used and their effect.

3 Choose one of the following tasks.

   a Imagine Billy and his family meet after the show. Write a dialogue between Jackie, Tony and Billy.

   b At the beginning of the show, Michael says "I wouldn't have missed it for the world." His partner doesn't know much of Michael's past yet and asks him for an explanation. Write down what Michael tells him.

   c A few days after the show Billy decides to write a letter to Mrs Wilkinson. He remembers how she once told him about Swan Lake. Write Billy's letter.

4 **Mediation:** After watching the movie, you discuss the ending of the film with a German friend. Give your opinion about the ending and reasons for your point of view. Focus on both the content of the scene and the filmic devices, as well as the music and the colours employed in this scene.

POST-VIEWING ACTIVITIES

A Cartoon

"It all started after he saw that 'Billy Elliot' movie on the telly."

1 Describe the cartoon.

2 Explain its message.

3 Discuss possible effects of movies on their viewers.

The British Coal Industry – Reading Comprehension

1 Read the text below. In paragraphs A–F, sentences have been left out.

1 Introduction: the Decline of King Coal

Since the Second World War, the British coal industry has undergone dramatic changes.

A

Commonly described as King Coal in the post war period, at the end of the century approached its status was far from regal, employing fewer than 10,000 workers (Table 1). This decline has been linked to changes in national energy policy, in the structure of the national energy market and in the unprecedented internationalisation of markets for coal.

2 Changing Markets for Coal

In 1947, when the coal mining industry was nationalised, with the exception of the road and marine transport sectors, coal provided the basis for all the energy needs of the country, industrial and domestic.

B

Ten years later the position of the coal industry and the coal districts had weakened considerably. The smog that had engulfed London and the Northern cities prompted the passing of Clean Air Acts in 1956 and 1968 with the creation of "smokeless zones" and the conversion of many homes and factories to fuels other than coal [...]. The dominance of coal was further weakened by the prospect of cheap oil, imported from the Middle East. The nuclear programme for electricity supply was seen to have an even greater significance. The early Magnox reactors seemingly promised a future of increasingly cheap fuel.

C

In this way, economically and politically, coal became relegated to a bygone era.

The effects of these changes were dramatic. Although the nuclear promise failed to materialise, cheap imported oil quickly replaced coal as a domestic and industrial fuel. Increasingly too, from the late 1960s, natural gas from the North Sea entered the market for fuel. As a consequence coal lost ground. In 1955, it accounted for 85.4% of UK energy consumption.

6 *regal* typical of a king or queen

22 *Magnox nuclear reactor* old-fashioned type of nuclear power reactor, designed and still in use in the UK

D

Although decline was halted in the 1970s and 1980s, it proved to be a short-lived reprieve. In this short space of time, therefore, the position of the National Coal Board (NCB) changed from that of monopoly producer to one amongst many in an increasingly competitive market-place.

In the 1960s, as the supply of coal was adjusted to the changes in the market, large numbers of collieries were closed, and over 400,000 miners left the industry

Durham represents a particularly clear example of this process. As the deep mines of the south-west of the coalfield were closed down, those on the east coast were expanded with new districts and faced being developed out under the North Sea. In a period of unbounded optimism, the Chairman of the Coal Board, Lord Robens, encouraged the miners to drive their tunnels eastward – "all the way to Norway". In contrast, in the west of the Durham coalfield, while some miners travelled to work in the expanding mines, many more left the industry and began to build new lives for themselves. Despite increased unemployment some jobs could still be found in the public sector and in the variety of light engineering and clothing and textile companies that had been attracted to the area

Moreover, despite the decline in the coal industry, the strikes of 1972 and 1974 to secure higher wages made clear that coal remained a critical fuel, particularly in the electricity supply industry (ESI). The increase in the price of oil, initially in 1973/4 and then again in 1979, brought this home to the coal miners and the National Union of Mineworkers (NUM), which set about organising to job security and higher wages for miners in the new conditions. [...]

4 Changing international markets and trade patterns and the political economy of Thatcherism

In the 1970s, the enormous expansion of steel production in Japan and the Pacific encouraged the exploration of new coking coal deposits in Australia and the transformation of South Africa into a major coal exporter. This coal (of high quality and low price) was increasingly mined through large open-cast sites, with surpluses offered for sale in Europe. In the early 1980s, under enormous pressure from the government to restructure its operations, British Steel switched its ordering policy away from British coking coals.

E

One by one the deep coking coal mines of Durham, Yorkshire and South Wales began to close.

This situation was accelerated toward a crisis by the determined policies of the newly elected Conservative Government, led by Margaret Thatcher. Coal, and the coal miners, were seen as the clearest example of a monopoly interest, subverting market forces and undermining the public good.

64 *surplus* an amount that is extra, more than you need

73 *subvert sth.* undermine/ threaten sth.

73 *public good* Allgemeinwohl

F

Furthermore, alternative sources of electricity supply were enthusiastically considered. Immediately following its election victory the government committed itself to the expansion of nuclear power.

Significantly the opposition to nuclear power involved the NUM, with its newly elected President Arthur Scargill as a key activist and debater. More generally – and not surprisingly – the NUM opposed Thatcherite energy policies and Scargill was determined to oppose colliery closures. This set the scene for the major strike of 1984–85. This mobilised large groups of people around the idea of supporting communities that had no future without coal mining. However, the determination of the Government ensured that the NUM would be defeated.

During the strike, significant amounts of coal were imported, especially along the east coast while electricity supplies were maintained by running the Magnox nuclear reactors at full capacity and through the dramatic replacement of coal with imported oil. This vulnerability of coal in its major (and previously secure) market presaged an uncertain future.

81 *colliery* mine

90 *presage sth.* foreshadow sth.

2 Looking at sentences 1–7 in the table below, choose the one which best fits each gap in the text. Write the letter of the missing sentences in the correct box. One gap has already been filled for you (F: sentence 2). There is one sentence you won't need.

1	By 1975 the share of coal in UK energy consumption had fallen to 36.2% (Table 2).	
2	Consequently developments in the international coal trade were welcomed and buyers encouraged to use this market to pressurise the coal monopoly.	F
3	As a result of its long history with coal, Britain's coal reserves have been depleted, and more than twice as much coal is now imported than produced.	
4	This was facilitated by a loosening of previous government restrictions on allowable levels of imports.	
5	The vision of increased use of these two fuels drew upon an increasingly optimistic view of economic change, technological development and social progress, one that was contrasted with a conservative traditional past.	
6	Consequently, in the 1940s and the early 1950s energy supply centred on the coal mines.	
7	From a position of dominance and seeming security in the national energy market, the coal mining industry has declined to a marginal position.	

facilitate sth. make sth. possible or easier

3 Outline the reasons for the decrease in coal production as explained in the text. In what way do tables 2 and 3 support these ideas?

4 Describe the trends presented in each table using the words on the right.

INFOBOX	Trends

Trends are the changes in facts and figures over a period of time. We can use different verbs and adjectives to describe trends:

Downward movement:
- decline
- decrease
- fall from ... to
- drop from ... to

Upward movement:
- increase
- rise
- grow
- climb

Figures can change ...
- slightly/slowly/gradually/minimally
- steadily/notably/considerably
- rapidly/suddenly/dramatically

Table 1 **Coal Mining in Britain – Anatomy of the Decline of Deep Mining**

Year	Collieries	Employment	Output (million tonnes)
1947	958	704 000	187
1957	650	699 000	213
1967	483	456 000	177
1977	238	242 000	108
1987	101	115 000	90
1997	15	8 000	39

Table 2 **UK Inland Consumption of Primary Fuels Percentage Shares (energy supplied basis)**

Fuel Sources	1950	1955	1960	1965	1970	1975	1980	1985	1990	1995	1996	1999
Coal	89.6	85.4	73.9	63.0	46.6	36.2	35.6	31.3	31.5	22.7	20.2	15.9
Petroleum	10.0	14.2	25.5	34.1	44.6	42.4	37.6	35.5	36.6	34.7	33.9	32.3
Natural Gas	--	--	--	0.4	5.3	17.2	21.8	25.0	23.6	31.9	35.6	40.8
Nuclear Electricity	--	--	0.4	2.3	3.3	4.0	4.8	8.0	7.6	9.7	9.6	8.4
Hydro Electricity	0.4	0.4	0.2	0.2	0.2	0.2	0.2	0.2	0.2	0.2	0.1	0.2
Electricity imports	--	--	--	--	--	--	--	--	0.5	0.6	0.6	0.5

Figures rounded to 1 decimal place [...]

Table 3 **UK Coal Consumption (million tonnes)**

Market Sector	1955	1973	1980	1990	1995	1996	1999
Power Stations	44	77	90	84	60	55	41
Industry*	50	13	8	6	4	4	3
Domestic/Commercial**	48	17	11	6	3	3	2
Railways	12	0	0	0	0	0	0
Coke Ovens	27	22	12	11	9	9	8
Manufactured Fuel Plants***	28	1	0	0	0	0	1
Other	2	3	3	1	1	1	1
Total	211	133	124	108	77	71	55

* – Includes colliery consumption
** – Includes Miners Coal and others
*** – includes gas works

Figures rounded to nearest million tonnes and includes consumption of stocks in some sectors

From: R. Hudson: *The Changing Geography of the British Coal Industry, 1947–97.* 2003

5 Explain the role of politics in the decrease in coal production.

The Miners' Strike – Internet Research and Presentation

1 Prepare a presentation about the miners' strike in Britain in 1984. Follow these steps:

a Brainstorm a list of questions concerning the strike that you can use as a guideline for your research.

b Do some research in order to find answers to your questions. The Website www.bbc.co.uk may offer some helpful information.

c Collect information, then structure it. Prepare some written materials to accompany your oral presentation (e.g. wall chart, hand-outs, electronic presentation tool …).

d Give your presentation. While listening to other presentations, evaluate them with the help of the criteria below.

Criteria for evaluating presentations

	well done (comments)	needs some work (comments/advice)
content: – quality of information – structure		
media: – variety – function – handling		
language: – fluency – variety of vocabulary		
body language: – gestures – facial expression		
interaction with the audience		

For or Against the Strike? – It's up for Discussion!

Watch the following sequences from chapters 5 and 7:
[00:23:25 – 00:24:03], [00:29:20 – 00:30:20] and [00:41:53 – 00:43:40].

1 Divide the class into two groups. As preparation for a discussion about strikes in general, one group collects arguments for strikes, the other against them. Use information from the film sequences and the texts above, but add your own ideas as well. One or two students should be prepared to lead the discussion.

2 Decide on the discussion format (debate, fish bowl, etc.) and, if necessary, on a statement to start with. Then hold the discussion.

Useful vocabulary:

Giving an opinion / Emphasizing	Agreeing / Defending one's point	Disagreeing / Arguing against sth.
In my opinion ... To my mind ... I am (strongly) convinced that ... I am of the opinion that ... I strongly believe that ... I would like to emphasize that ... There is strong evidence that ...	I (totally) agree (with you). Exactly. Absolutely. That is definitely true (but ...). You are certainly right (but ...). You have a point there (but ...). I see your point (but ...).	I (completely) disagree (with you on ...). I'm not so sure about that. I am sorry but I don't agree with you here. I'd doubt that ... I'm afraid I don't think/believe that ... I think you are mistaken when ... I would question that argument.

3 What is your personal opinion about strikes as a means of exerting influence on political decisions? Write a comment of about 200 words.

Parallele – Lufthansa / Bahn

A Review – Reading and Writing

Who would want to see a movie about a miner's son in Northern England whose life is forever changed one day when he stumbles upon a ballet class on his way to boxing lessons? Well, the answer is simple: anyone looking to see one of the year's best films.

Billy Elliot is the kind of feel-good motion picture that only the British film industry seems capable of producing (think, 1997's *Brassed Off*). Although he must keep his growing interest in the world of ballet a secret from his widowed father (Gary Lewis) and overbearing older brother, Tony (Jamie Draven), 11-year-old Billy (Jamie Bell) discovers that dance is more than a means of self-expression, it becomes a passion.

He is encouraged by the exacting instructor Mrs Wilkinson (Julie Walters) who recognizes the lad's potential and works with him with the goal of landing an audition at the Royal Ballet School in London. After his father and brother become aware of his secret and ban him from ballet class, Billy has to make an important decision – to remain in his oppressive hometown or escape to London to pursue his dream.

Newcomer Jamie Bell, himself a dancer since the age of six, delivers a stirring performance as the title character. Bell skillfully uses his body to articulate Billy's inner longings through his awkward, unpolished movements and also handles the dramatic aspects of the role well. Julie Walters is terrific as the blasé dance teacher who recognizes Billy's gifts and offers to train him. Gary Lewis as Billy's dad takes what could easily have been a stock character and makes him almost heroic. When he makes a decision that goes against his principles but would guarantee a better life for his youngest child, it is dramatic peak in the film.

Award-winning stage director Stephen Daldry makes an auspicious feature film debut at the helm of Billy Elliot. He and screenwriter Lee Hall have managed to avoid the clichés that torpedoed the similarly-themed *Bootmen* and delivers a superlative comedy-drama. Daldry's ease with the camera, his ability to shape scenes and focus on the action and his success with the actors bode well for a long future behind the camera.

Some might quibble over the plot and themes because they seemingly have been done to death, but far from turning them into recycled pap, Daldry and company have made an enjoyable, exhilarating and just plain fun movie.

From: www.hollywood.com

6 *Brassed Off* film about the closure of a coalmine, which might also put an end to the miners' brass band

11 *exacting (adj)* demanding a lot of work and effort

21 *blasé (here)* indifferent and slightly arrogant

23 *stock character* ordinary, standard character

27 *helm* handle or wheel used for steering a ship

29 *Bootmen* film about a charismatic young tap dancer who works in a steel mill

31 *bode well for sth.* be a good sign for sth.

33 *pap (infml)* worthless, unoriginal material

1 Choose one sentence from the review that you like best or do not like at all. Explain your choice to a partner.

2 Comment on the critic's opinion of the movie.

3 Use the FILM STUDIES: EXTRAS section (p. 55) to learn about the typical structure of a film review. Write your own review of the film.

A Review – Mediation

1 You want to watch a movie with an English exchange partner. He liked *Billy Elliot* because of the music and dance, and the way it deals with being different. You suggest watching *Happy Feet*. Use the review below to summarize the storyline and convince your partner.

Der Pinguin-Junge Mumble kämpft gegen Konformitätsdruck und die Überfischung der Ozeane. George Millers Animationsfilm ist klug geschrieben, schön anzuschauen und kann mit einem Allstar-Cast aufwarten.

Als ich den Trailer zu „Happy Feet" sah, dachte ich: „Schon wieder Pinguine. Und jetzt singen sie auch noch? Himmel, Herrgott! Wer will denn so etwas sehen?" Dann allerdings, nachdem ich den Film tatsächlich gesehen hatte: „Eigentlich gar nicht so übel. Wie konnte ich nur so voller Vorurteile sein?" Und das kam so: Der kleine Kaiserpinguin Mumble (Elijah Wood) ist nicht wie seine Artgenossen. Die trällern einen Gassenhauer nach dem anderen (mit Vorliebe jüngere R'n'B-Hits), aber wenn Mumble singt, klingt es, als würde man ein Huhn erdrosseln. Dafür kann Mumble tanzen wie Fred Astaire selig. Dumm nur, dass man damit am Nordpol nicht glücklich wird: Die Währung bei Pinguins heißt Wohlklang, und wer bloß „Happy Feet" hat, zieht den Kürzeren. „It's just not penguin," meint der Vater und fordert seinen Sohn auf, nicht so nervös von einem Bein aufs andere zu springen – Konformitätsdruck, kennt man ja.

Doch Mumble mag sich nicht anpassen. Und als ihm die Klassenkameraden vorwerfen, mit seinem Gekrächze ihre Abschlussfeier zu ruinieren, nimmt er Reißaus. Er landet bei einer Gang von Latino-Pinguinen, die nicht nur herrlich witzig sind (ihr Anführer wird gesprochen von Robin Williams, der nur noch als Pinguin auftreten sollte), sondern auch Mumbles Tanzkünste zu schätzen wissen. Singen lernt der Junge auch hier nicht, aber am Ende wird er den Pinguinen mit seinem Tanzen das Überleben sichern.

Eine Prämisse wie diese – ungefähr: „Die Reise der Pinguine" trifft „Riverdance" – lässt vernünftige Menschen schaudern. Aber Regisseur George Miller [...] und seine Drehbuchschreiber haben „Happy Feet" mit genug Stars (neben Wood und Williams hört man etwa Brittany Murphy, Hugh Jackman, Nicole Kidman, Hugo Weaving) und witzigen Dialogen ausgestattet, um Kinder und Erwachsene bei Stange zu halten. Schön anzusehen ist das alles sowieso. Manche Szenen wirken fotorealistisch, andere verbreiten eine gespenstische Stimmung.

Seine zwei zentralen Anliegen – Toleranz für alternative Lebensformen und Respekt der Natur gegenüber – machen dem Film Ehre, er schafft sich damit aber auch ein erzählerisches Dilemma. Wenn in der zweiten Hälfte die Überfischung der Ozeane das Thema ist, wird Mumbles Tanzen nebensächlich und ist am Ende mehr schlecht als recht mit dem neuen Strang der Geschichte verwoben. In Anbetracht der restlichen Qualitäten dieser computeranimierten Öko-Fabel ist das allerdings eine lässliche Sünde.

From: www.cineman.ch

EXAM TASKS

Tasks similar to the following might occur in written exams. You can choose one or more from each section to prepare for exams.

I Comprehension

1 Summarize the film in about 150 words.

2 State Billy's dilemma.

3 Outline how life in County Durham is affected by the strike.

II Analysis

1 Explain Jackie's aversion to Billy's hobby.

2 Contrast the Wikinsons' and the Elliots' lives with regard to class in the UK.

3 Analyse the director's use of music in the film.

4 Examine how Billy expresses emotion in the film.

5 Examine the function of the minor characters in the movie. Focus at least on Debbie, George and Billy's grandmother.

6 Compare Jackie's and Billy's attitudes towards dancing.

7 Analyse the significance of stereotypes in the film.

III Comment/Composition/Creative Writing

1 Comment on many critics' description of Billy Elliot as a "feel-good movie".

2 Assess the effectiveness of striking.

3 Evaluate Jackie's role as a father.

4 Michael and Billy meet after the performance of Swan Lake at the end of the movie. Write their dialogue.

5 After Tony has seen Billy's performance he tells his wife about it. Write their dialogue.

6 After the performance Billy has got the chance to speak to the audience about his career. Write his speech.

SELECTED TERMS FOR FILM ANALYSIS

Camera range/kinds of shot	The distance between camera and object
close shot	In a close shot a person's face, shoulders and part of his/her arm are shown.
close-up 	An entire human face from chin or lower neck to top of head fills the frame. Shows the finest nuances of expression.
extreme close-up 	Parts of the face (or object) fill the entire frame.
full shot 	Includes the entire body of a character and not much else. The full shot is used to emphasize action and the constellation of characters.
long shot 	Characters and surroundings are shown from a distance and in their entirety. It is usually used to introduce a new setting (see establishing shot) to show characters in relation to the action, to show movement over large distances, or to juxtapose different characters within one frame.
medium shot 	Characters and surroundings are shown at a moderate size, with characters seen from mid-body up. It is usually chosen to show one or two characters in action.

Camera perspective	
establishing shot	A **long shot** that establishes a setting, scene or mood; frequently used at the beginning of a scene.
over-the-shoulder shot	A shot taken with the camera placed behind a character who is only partially seen, looking over his/her shoulder. Usually used in dialogue scenes, showing the dialogue partner from the second character's point of view.
point-of-view shot	Also known as 'subjective camera'. A shot taken with the camera placed approximately where the characters' eyes would be in order to depict a scene from the visual or emotional perspective of one of the characters.
shot/reverse shot **reverse-angle shot** 	A **shot/reverse shot** is an **over-the-shoulder shot** followed by a **reverse-angle shot**. A **reverse-angle shot** is a shot in which the angle is opposite to that in the preceding shot.
Camera angle	
eye-level shot/ **straight-on angle** 	A shot filmed at eye level.
high-angle shot 	A shot filmed from above the object; may be used to diminish the character's importance.
low-angle shot 	Filmed from below the object, a **low-angle shot** may be used to underline the importance or power of a character or object. Shown as a **point-of-view shot**, it indicates fear or respect on the part of the character viewing a particular scene.

Camera movement	
crane shot 	A shot filmed from a crane that can move the camera in any direction. It is almost always linked to another movement of the camera, such as a **pan** or **tilt**, in which case it becomes a compound movement.
hand-held camera	A filming technique in which the camera is held by the operator during a take.
pan/panning shot 	The camera moves horizontally from left to right or vice versa (**pan** right or **pan** left). A **panning shot** is often used to follow a character's movement or to indicate a **point-of-view shot** with the character looking around or searching for something.
tilt/tilt shot	The camera moves vertically upward or downward. A **tilt shot** is often used to indicate height or follow a character or object moving up or downwards, e.g. a leaf dropping.
tracking shot 	Camera movement in which the entire camera is moved either forward, backward, laterally, or in a circular or irregular pattern. The camera is placed on a movable device (a camera dolly) moving along pre-laid tracks or is moved freely along a level surface (hand-held camera or steady cam). In a **tracking shot**, the camera range may either remain constant, following along next to or behind a moving character or object, or it may be used to get closer to or further away from the target object in a manner similar to a **zoom** shot. Usually used to indicate steady movement through the setting, e.g. indicating a character running or two characters walking together.
zoom 	The stationary camera appears to approach a character or object by **zooming in** or to move farther away by **zooming out**.
Editing terms	**The arrangement of shots in a structured sequence**
cross-cutting/ parallel action	Also known as parallel editing. An editing technique that alternates shots of two or more actions occurring in different places at the same time. Usually used to follow multiple plot lines, to compare or to juxtapose different actions or settings, or to show different reactions to a particular event.
cut	Transition from one shot to another. The most basic editing technique for connecting two shots within a scene and between scenes.

jump-cut	A (very) abrupt transition from one shot to another eleminating one strip of action and creating an effect of disorientation or rapid movement.
match cut	A technique in which two shots are linked by the same acting or by some form of visual parallelism. The two shots seem to continue uninterrupted, e.g. one door closing and then another door opening. **Match cuts** can be used to underline a connection between two separate elements. Often used to create a smooth flow between two scenes or, if using the same character in the action, to mark the passing of time.
dissolve	A transition between two shots created by gradually overlapping the last shot of a scene with the first shot of the next scene. This is done by superimposing a **fade-out** onto a **fade-in** of equal length. Often this transition is used to underline the connection between two scenes or to indicate a change of location or the passing of time.
fade-in **fade-out**	A transition between two shots. The last image of one scene gradually disappears from the screen (**fade-out**) to be replaced by a monochrome screen, and the first shot of the next scene gradually brightens from a blank screen to the whole image (**fade-in**). Often used to indicate a passing of time (e.g. from night to day), or to mark the beginning and end of a dream sequence (**flashback** or **flash-forward**).
flashback	A filmed sequence that goes back in narrative time to show events that took place earlier than the present-time of the film. Usually used to provide expository material and to underline the feelings and motives of characters.
flash-forward	A filmed sequence that moves forward in narrative time to show events that take place later than the present-time of the film. Usually used to underline the presence of an omniscient narrator, a **flash-forward** shows the consequences of a certain action that the characters are still unaware of. It gives the audience the impression of knowing more than the characters.
Additional film terms	
arc shot	Camera movement in which the entire camera moves around a subject or object in a circle.
backlighting	Filming a person or event against a background of light, e.g. the sun. It may produce an idealized, sometimes romantic effect.
camera operator	The person behind the camera(s); in major productions, the head of the camera team is usually called the director of photography.
cast	All actors who appear in a film.

clapboard (US)/ **clapperboard** (GB) 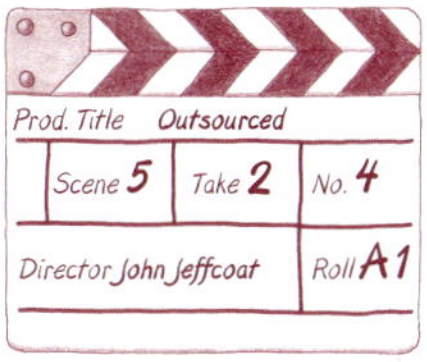 	A small board which gives information about a film: e.g. the director, the director of photography, the scene, take number, date and time. It is filmed at the beginning of each take. It helps to identify all takes and cuts down continuity errors.
credits	The list of people who were involved in the making of a film or television programme.
director	The person responsible for the artistic production of a film, involving all its creative elements, e.g. camerawork, editing, and the actors' interpretation of their roles.
editor	(verb: edit) The person responsible for putting the camera shots together and arranging them into a finished product.
fade	Transition between two shots. The last image gradually disappears from the screen (**fade-out**) to be replaced by a monochrome screen, and the first shot of the next screen gradually brightens from a blank screen to the whole image (**fade-in**).
footage	A length of film made for TV or cinema.
frame	A single image of the film.
insert (shot)	A detail shot which quickly gives visual information necessary to understand the meaning of a scene, e.g. a newspaper page or a physical detail.
lighting	The creation of controlled illumination upon a scene or object to be filmed and thus the ultimate tool of the cinematographer. Light sources may be natural or artificial or both. If natural, the light may be directed onto the scene by reflecting devices. If artificial, it is of course aimed at the specific target area designated by the director of photography and channelled through the use of such devices as cookies, flags, and doors. The light may also be diffused or it may be sharply focused. If, as might be said, cinematography is painting with light, lighting is the palette which the painter uses. Though methods for lighting a scene are highly varied, the one most commonly used in conventional practice is known as the 'Three-Point Lighting System'.
high-key lighting **low-key lighting**	The intensity and sharpness of light and corresponding shadow (or lack of this) which illuminates a scene is described as being either **high** or **low key**. This is true irrespective of whether the film is monochromatic or in colour. Lighting that creates comparatively little contrast between the light and dark areas of the shot is **high-key**, lighting that creates strong contrast between the light and dark areas of the shot is **low-key lighting**.
location	See: set.

mise-en-scène	Literally translated from French, the phrase means 'put upon the stage'; otherwise known simply as 'staging'. In film-making the term has come to mean the totality of how the director designs and sets in motion a given scene. All films use essentially the same techniques and processes. However, each individual film employs all of the variable elements of production provided by the technology available in its own distinct way. The elements generally used to define and analyse **mise-en-scène** are: setting, actor placement, actor movement, actor interpretation (ideally, but not always a collaboration between director and actor), camera movement, costumes and make-up.
motion picture/movie	US and Canadian terms for film.
producer	The person responsible for the overall organization, especially the financing and marketing, of a film or television production.
scene	A shot or series of shots that deal with a single action (see also **sequence**).
score	Film music.
screenplay	The script of a film or television show, usually including dialogue as well as rough descriptions of the setting, camera distance, camera movements, etc.
sequence	A part of a film dealing with one or more scenes that form a single continuous episode.
set	The site or location where a film is being shot.
shot	A single piece of film, however long or short, taken by a single camera without cuts.
soundtrack	The audio equivalent of the picture or image track, the **soundtrack** contains all the audio information which accompanies the film: dialogue, music, sound effects, etc.
still	A single photograph or shot from a film.
storyboard	A **storyboard** is a useful tool in the creation of any media production. It is a series of sketches or still photographs that show how the different shots might look when filmed. It almost looks like a comic book of the film.
take	A single attempt to film a shot. Though sometimes confused with **shot**, there can in fact be an unlimited number of takes of the same shot until either the director is satisfied or the producer calls a halt.
top shot	Extreme **high-angle shot** where the camera looks straight down.
voice-over	An off-screen voice that gives the audience necessary background information. It is often used in documentaries. In a narrative film, this technique often implies a first-person or omniscient narrator's point of view.
wipe	Transitional device in which shot B seemingly moves in either screen direction across shot A, thus effectively wiping off shot A and replacing it.

WORKING WITH A FILM VIEWING LOG

You are probably used to keeping a reading log when studying a novel. When studying a film, it is even more important to take notes during the viewing process for future reference, as it is more difficult to go back to different parts of the film.

Before viewing
Find out all you can about the film you are going to see:

What genre does it belong to (e.g. feature film, documentary, video clip, newscast, commercial)? What country does it come from? When was it made? Are you going to see it in the original language (with or without subtitles), or is it a dubbed version? Was it made for television or for the cinema?

While viewing
Pay close attention to how visual and audio elements influence your reaction to the film:

- **Characters:** How does the film show you who the main characters are? What information do you get about them? What is their relationship to each other? What impression do they make on you, and why? Watch for facial expressions and body language that may convey important signals.
- **Setting:** How does the film let you know where the plot is set? What impression do you get of the setting? How do colour, music, lighting, background noise contribute to this impression?
- **Plot:** Is the plot introduced gradually (e.g. while the titles are being shown) or does the story begin in the middle and make the viewer draw conclusions based on indirect clues? Does it use flashbacks (or flash-forwards), or is the story told chronologically? Does the point of view of one character dominate, or does the film jump from one character to another? Is there one main plot, or does the film tell a series of loosely connected episodes? Are special effects used, and if so, to what effect?
- **Information:** Particularly in a documentary film, consider how the information presented to the viewer. Does the director use music to appeal to the emotions and convince his audience? Is slow motion used? If so, when and why?

Using a viewing log can help you to keep track of what you notice while watching a film or video sequence.

Your viewing log might look like the one below, but feel free to choose different categories to fit your own purposes:

What? (sequence/ scene)	When/Where?	Who?	Filmic devices	Comments/ Questions

After viewing

Go over your viewing log again and add information or comments. Think about your overall response to the film:

What emotions does the film arouse, and through what means? Do you identify with one or more of the characters, and if so, why? Does the film try to make you take sides, or does it encourage you to draw your own conclusions? Discuss these questions with others who have seen the film and analyse the reasons for your reactions. If possible, re-examine sequences/ scenes that provoked conflicting views and discuss why you respond to them in different ways.

HOW TO WRITE A FILM REVIEW

A film review is a written text that provides information about a film. It is intended either to recommend the film in question or to discourage people from seeing it. It can also help people to form their own opinion of the film.

- Start by considering the various elements which make up a film: the characters, the setting and the plot.
- Say what the film is about, giving the title, genre, name of the director and when it was made. Among other things, you may want to include awards and the names of actors.
- Give background information on the film and the director.
- Give specific information on what the film is about and provide a short summary without giving away the ending (unless this is explicitly required). You should aim to make your audience curious and encourage them to watch the film themselves rather than give everything away.
- Finish the review with your personal opinion (on the actors' performance or the adaptation of the novel, for instance), give reasons for your opinion and say whether you would recommend it or not.
- Remember to structure your review into three main parts:
  - an introduction with a catchy first sentence,
  - a main body outlining your main points (one per paragraph),
  - a conclusion summarizing the points made.

Useful vocabulary:

The film was produced/directed by ...
It is set in / covers a period of / tells the story of ...
The main characters are ...
The story is rather weak/boring/unconvincing.
The storyline is entertaining/gripping/fascinating/clever.
I can thoroughly recommend the film.

HOW TO ANALYSE FILM STILLS

When analysing a film still, concentrate on the following aspects:

- the content and setting of the still: what can be seen in the picture and where? When and where is the action set?

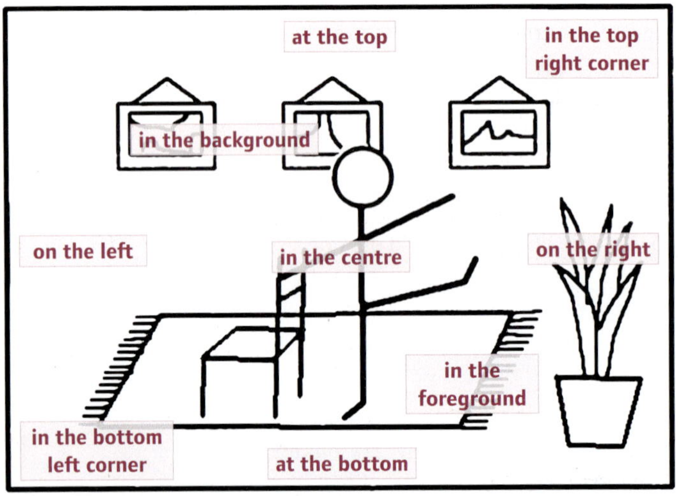

- the proportion of objects in the still; their arrangement in the foreground or background
- the camera angle and the perspective from which the still is taken
- the lighting and the colours of the still
- the overall impression: what impression is created by the above aspects?

Useful vocabulary:

The field size is a The camera takes a	long medium close …	shot	
The persons are The scene is …	filmed	from at	below above eye-level

1 Lend me your eyes: choose any still from the film and describe its major features to a partner. Make sure that your partner cannot see the original picture. Your partner draws a sketch while listening to your description. Then compare both pictures.